IMAGES
of England

KINGSTON UPON HULL

THE SECOND SELECTION

High Street, formerly Hull Street, has changed beyond recognition at this point. This 1905 view by Hull photographers Parrish & Berry Ltd was taken looking north along High Street from its junction with Blackfriargate. One of Hull's lost pubs, the tiny Old Harbour Inn, can be seen on the centre-left of the photograph. Sadly none of the buildings shown survive today.

IMAGES
of England

KINGSTON UPON HULL
THE SECOND SELECTION

Paul Gibson

TEMPUS

Tempus Publishing Limited
The Mill, Brimscombe Port,
Stroud, Gloucestershire, GL5 2QG

ISBN 0 7524 2607 9

Typesetting and origination by
Tempus Publishing Limited
Printed in Great Britain by
Midway Colour Print, Wiltshire

This book is dedicated to my mother, Annie Lillian Gibson, (1918–1989)

Acknowledgements

I should like to thank Ken Grayson for the use of two postcards from his collection (KG); the staff of the Hull Local Studies Library; Ken Jackson of the Memory Lane Photographic Archive, Hessle Road, Hull for the use of eight photographs from this collection (ML); Christopher Ketchell for his work to promote and protect our architectural and social heritage, proof-reading, and for the use of three photographs (CJK); Terry Mills for the use of a postcard from his collection (TM); Kevin Rymer for the use of eight postcards and photographs from his collection (KR); Gail Thornton for her patience and services whilst I sat, open-mouthed, staring at a computer; Rhonda Thornton for the use of a family photograph (RT); Martin Taylor of the Kingston upon Hull City Archives for the use of three photographs (HCA) and Graham Wilkinson for proof reading.

Contents

Bibliography

Aldridge, Carolyn Hull City Museums & Art Galleries with the Hutton Press, Beverley
    Images of Victorian Hull –F.S. Smith's Drawings of the Old Town, 1989.
Associated British Ports, London *The Port of Hull Handbook*, 2001.
Barnard, Robert (CD Rom) HCLHU *Hull Times Index 1857-1945*, 2001.
Brown & Sons, Hull *Hull Public Baths Official Handbook*, c. 1920
Curry, Robert Hull College, Hutton Press & Humberside County Council, Beverley
    Last Complete Performance – In Memory of Hull's Cinemas, 1992.
Davis, Paul Brown & Sons, Hull *The Old Friendly Societies of Hull*, 1926.
Gibson, Paul privately published Hull *Desirable Abodes for all Parties Visiting Hull – The Waterworks
    Street Pubs*, 1999.
Gillett, Edward and Macmahon, Kenneth University of Hull Press *A History of Hull*, 1989.
Hall, Ivan and Elizabeth Wm Sessions Ltd, York *Georgian Hull*, 1978-79.
Johnson & Sons, Hull *Souvenir of the Opening of the New North Bridge*, 1931.
Ketchell, Christopher Hutton Press Ltd, Beverley *Postcards of Old Hull*, 1997.
Ketchell, Christopher Hull City Museums & Art Galleries with the Hutton Press, Beverley
    Images of Victorian Hull – F.S. Smith's Drawings of Hull 2, 1990.
Ketchell, Christopher HCLHU *Tremendous Activity in the Old Town – Demolitions Loss List
    1943-1988*, 1989.
Ketchell, Christopher HCLHU *The Beverley Road Walk*, 1997.
Ketchell, Christopher HCLHU *Spring Bank Cemetery Walk*, 1999.
Ketchell, Christopher HCLHU *Hull School Board Schools*, Work in Progress, 2001.
Ketchell, Christopher HCLHU *Pearson Park, the Peoples Park*, 1995.
Kimberley, Stephen Humberside College of Higher Education, Local History Archives Unit, Hull
    Humberside in the First World War, 1988.
Markham, John Highgate Publications, Beverley *Streets of Hull – A History of Their Names*, 1990.
Morgan, Kenneth Guild Publishing, London *The Oxford Illustrated History of Britain*, 1984.
Neave, David Hull City Museums and Art Galleries and the Hutton Press, Beverley
    Lost Churches & Chapels of Hull, 1991.
Needler, Raymond Hutton Press, Beverley *Needlers of Hull*, 1993.
Oxford University Press, London *The Victoria History of the Counties of England: York East Riding
    Volume I: The City of Kingston Upon Hull*, 1969.
Pevsner, Nikolaus and Neave, David Penguin Books, London *The Buildings of England: Yorkshire
    – York & the East Riding*, 1995.
Reckitt, Basil N. Brown & Sons, Hull *The History of Reckitt & Sons Ltd*, 1952.
Sheahan, James Joseph publisher John Green, Beverley *History of the Town and Port of Kingston
    upon Hull* 2nd ed., 1866.
Smith, John E. Hutton Press Ltd, Beverley *Hull in the 1950s*, 1994.
Strafford, Robert Hull College Local History Unit (HCLHU) *Lost Property (Police Boxes &
    Cabmen's Shelters of Hull)*, 1998.
Suthers, Terence EP Publishing Ltd, Wakefield *Hull Old & New*, 1975.
Thompson, Michael Hutton Press, Beverley *Hull Docklands – An Illustrated History of the Port of
    Hull*, 1990.
Wilkinson, Graham *Landlord*, Work in Progress, 2002.
Wrigglesworth, Edmund ed. Mr Pye Books, Howden, *Brown's Illustrated Guide to Hull
    (1891)*, 1992.
Trade directories, various.
www.federationoffishfriers.co.uk/history *Federation of Fish Friers*.
The Athlete, 1889.
The Hull Graphic, 1907.

Introduction

Collecting old photographs can become a depressing pastime if you're not careful. By their very nature old photographs tend to feature subjects which are often no longer with us, such as churches, schools, pubs etc., many of which will have been demolished since the photograph was taken. Undeterred I have been an avid collector of photographs and other items of Hull related ephemera for some years.

Another pitfall of collecting is that you often simply store the material away in albums, boxes, files and only you and a few friends see the pictures. The likelihood is that they will be hidden away forever. Q. When is a picture not a picture? A. When no one can see it! The temptation to squirrel away a valuable collection is one to which many collectors fall foul and I too fell into this trap for a time, but have endeavoured over the past few years to make my collections available for the benefit of others. Perhaps if others see what a fine and handsome place Hull used to be, they may be a little more thoughtful and sympathetic when it comes to its future redevelopment. I hope that by publishing my collection in this way it may persuade others to open theirs too so that others can appreciate them.

And so to the images: I have tried to avoid presenting page after page of familiar scenes from the city centre that have already been published. Some, now spoilt, areas of the city and many lost buildings do however deserve another look now and again. When I have selected some familiar scenes, I have attempted to use photographs that will be new to most readers and unseen in other publications. The majority of the images are from my own collections, with occasional gems loaned from friends and fellow collectors. The images show the diversity of life in and around Hull from the 1890s to the end of the Second World War. I have sought to show the people of Hull as well as the streets, which in many cases have changed little.

My particular favourites include shop fronts and images with gatherings of people, whether a grand parade, or a candid scene in a back street. Pub groups or outings are another genre I enjoy and this stems from my fondness for pubs in general! Many of the shop businesses featured in this book have become a rare sight indeed in the twenty-first century. Some of these shops were an entertainment in themselves – almost a day out. I have fond memories of the shops in and around Charles Street and Waterloo Street where I was born and spent most of my early years.

The history and origins of Hull are well documented in other volumes mentioned in the bibliography. This book is a pictorial glimpse of life in the city in days when heavy traffic meant only one motorcar and a few trams clogging up Monument Bridge, when you could walk along the centre of Beverley Road without fear of being run over and children could play safely around the trees that lined the centre of Spring Bank. Words like 'dual carriageway' and 'motorway' were not in the dictionary and there was a pub in every street and virtually full employment. I would give a lot for a week around Hull with my camera in the year 1900!

Fortunately, Hull has been blessed with many gifted photographers over the years, both professional and amateur. Photography was first 'sold' to the public of Hull in newspaper advertisements of 1843 and developed steadily, until in 1863 for example, there were sixteen professional photographers listed in one trade directory. By the turn of the twentieth century that number had more than doubled. Sadly very few very early photographs have survived and it was not until the picture postcard boom of the Edwardian era that streets were photographed on a regular basis by local photographers.

The sending and collecting of postcards became the biggest hobby in England for a short period of time. It is those photographers who produced photographic picture postcards that we have to thank for the hundreds of views of our streets, many of which have fortunately survived in family collections. The city of Hull had two major companies producing picture postcards, William J. Wellsted & Son of Paragon Street; and probably the most prolific, Parrish & Berry

Ltd of Waltham Street, Hull. Both firms produced huge numbers of images, Wellsteds from the 1880s onwards, and Parrish & Berry from 1901. These two companies produced many of the views in this book. Several others are by local jobbing photographers, who possibly only lasted a year or so in what was then a very competitive market. As far as we know none of these photographers have left any records of their business or any of their negatives. So those postcards that have survived are now extremely rare and are keenly sought by collectors all over the world. Many of the views they recorded have rarely, if ever, been previously published. They often show aspects of life and society that would never have been seen without them. These images show how we owe them a huge debt of gratitude.

The surviving Dock Office buildings of around 1868 (now the Maritime Museum) to the right of this picture are the only clue to its location. All of the buildings shown in the centre of this view, from around 1870 by W.J. Wellsted & Son, were demolished for the construction of Victoria Square. The Wilberforce statue was moved in 1935 to its present site outside the Hull College at the eastern end of Queens Gardens.

One
The Old Town

The southern end of Queen Street, which runs from Humber Street to Nelson Street, is not an ancient thoroughfare and was only constructed around 1802 on land reclaimed from the River Humber. It was one of many new streets laid out, including Wellington Street and Nelson Street, which were built upon spoil from the creation of Humber Dock to the west. By the time of this view, of around 1905 which looks north towards Market Place, it had become one of Hull's main shopping areas. The Oberon public house (now the Cask & Cutter) can be seen to the right of the picture opposite the huge gaslamps of Woodruffe's Royal Hotel on the immediate left. Also on the left, at the north side of Wellington Street, are the former offices of seed-merchant's Dixon & Co. The four-storey block, which survives today, is constructed on the site of a theatre, built in 1827, named the Apollo.

This lady stands in the entrance to a court on the west side of High Street known as Temple's Entry. Although very little evidence exists to confirm this, some of the buildings shown may formerly have been the rooms of a sixteenth-century timber-framed inn known as the Kings Head. Despite protests at the time the historic building was demolished around 1905.

The Victoria Pier was the place to be on a sunny weekend or evening in Edwardian Hull. To us it might be a scene in a television costume drama but the horse-drawn cabs, the steamboat and the newly built cabmen's shelter were all very much part of everyday life. In this 1907 view very few people are promenading but the long shadows suggest it was late evening.

Hull was one of those unfortunate cities that had the misfortune to be bombed in both world wars. Few now realise that Zeppelins dropped bombs on the city in 1915 and 1916. Queen Street was one of several to be affected and amongst those properties damaged were those of Blenkin & Son, saddlers of Nos 76 and 77, which received a direct hit in March 1916.

Market Place is a confusing title as, unlike most towns and cities, Hull's Market Place no longer holds the market. By the time of this photograph, around 1905, it had become the point of transit for many carriers whose carts can be seen manoeuvring around 'King Billy'. In the distance can be seen De Wets Waxworks, No. 50 Market Place, occupying what is now the forecourt of the Corn Exchange public house.

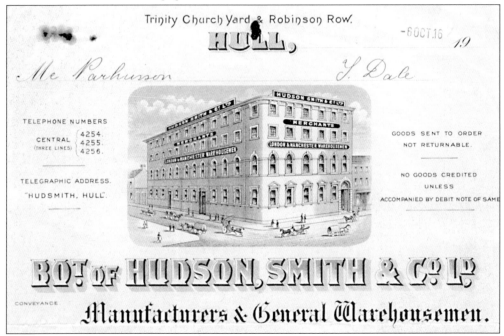

Stationery just isn't what it used to be; the importance of your company was reflected in the quality of your letterhead. This fine example dated 6 October 1916 has a decorative heading that takes up two thirds of the paper! Artistic licence has been used to exaggerate the size of Hudson Smith & Co. Ltd in relation to the size of passing pedestrians and vehicles.

Police and young men search the ruins of what, prior to 6 June 1915, had been the premises of drapers Edwin Davis & Co. Ltd. Their store at Nos 45-49 Market Place was completely destroyed. Twenty-five people were killed and around a hundred more injured in this first air raid on Hull by German airships.

Number 17 Market Place was owned by woollen merchants Lawton & Bowron. This conveyance dated 3 March 1908 records the sale of 'two dozen mufflers, one dozen assorted Eton caps and one gross of felt buckles for the sum of fifteen shillings'. Again the letterhead artist has been employed to amplify the appearance of their quite modest shop which occupied the corner of Church Lane.

At the junction with Silver Street the Market Place ends and Lowgate begins. This busy junction, shown here in a photograph of around 1907 by Wellsted & Son, is looking north. On the right of the picture a LNER cart discharges parcels at the receiving office of the Hull & Barnsley Railway.

St Mary's church, Lowgate. This view is taken from the south when the former Yorkshire Insurance Co. buildings at No. 30 Lowgate (by Brodrick & Lowther), were constructed. The present office block replaced the Victorian offices in 1974 and similarly obscures the view. Wellsted & Son reproduced this photograph as a postcard view around 1905.

In contrast to the drawing of Lawton & Bowron's premises, the former Midland Bank at the corner of Silver Street is genuinely huge and does tower over the public. Its sturdy features gave the saving public a subliminal sense of security. Most of the buildings in the picture survive but the bank is now a bar and meeting place for revellers around town, dispensing with their savings, rather than depositing them.

Another bank dominates the junction of Trinity House Lane, Whitefriargate, the Land of Green Ginger and Silver Street, in this 1904 photograph by Parrish & Berry of Hull. Beyond the bank in Whitefriargate, is the former George Hotel with obligatory huge gaslamp over the

door. The hotel no longer exists but its former tap and coach entrance survive to the rear, now known as the George public house, fronting the Land of Green Ginger.

Whitefriargate was originally part of an ancient route called Aldgate which went through the centre of the town along the line of Whitefriargate, Silver Street and Scale Lane. It had always been a trading area and by the time of this photograph, taken in 1931, it was a major shopping centre and remains as such today. Changes in fashion and transport are all that is different from the previous view some twenty-five years earlier.

The old Monument Bridge or Junction Bridge over the entrance to Queens Dock became too small for the increases size of vehicles and amount of traffic in modern Hull. The new larger bridge is shown in the final stages of construction and testing in this photographic postcard, before becoming operational early in 1906. To the rear are the former Dock Offices, now the Maritime Museum.

Another of Hull's many Edwardian photographers was Frank Overton, who took this image of the almost completed bridge. A feature of the improved bridge was the facility for electric trams to pass over it easily using the specially modified catenary poles for their wires. Many people today will not be aware that the area known as Monument Bridge did at one time actually have a monument and a bridge.

Alfred Gelder Street was one of many new roads which cut through the city centre to ease traffic flow in the early years of the twentieth century. Taken from the upper floors of the former Dock Offices around 1930, this photograph shows the former Queens Dock in the course of being filled-in from the eastern end and the goods transit sheds, used by off-loading ships, along Guildhall Road at the side of the dock.

The message on the back of this postcard reads, 'I dare say if I keep on singing I shall be finding lodgings in this splendid building'. Splendid as the old police station at the corner of Parliament Street and Alfred Gelder Street was, it was still almost completely demolished in January 1979, following its sale to the Littlewood's chain. Tragically, only a small part of the former Parliament Street entrance survives.

Hull's streets were as filled with advertising material a hundred years ago as they are now, possibly even more so. But where would you have gone to have your business advertised? Perhaps to Bowland & Co. advertising contractors. This letterhead served as an advertisement for their own services, with advertisements of a different kind to those seen on today's hoardings. When was the last time you saw a sandwich-board?

The old Town Hall of 1866 by Cuthbert Brodrick dominates this view, *c.* 1907. To the right of the picture is the City Hotel, built around 1905 by W.S. Walker. The old Town Hall was demolished in 1912 and the east end of the new Guildhall, constructed between 1912 and 1916, took its place. To the immediate right of the Town Hall in Hanover Square can be seen one of Hull's lost cabmen's shelters.

Hull's former general post office has recently been converted to the excellent Three John Scotts public house, a snooker hall and the City Exchange apartments. In its former existence it was the hub of Hull's postal services. This 1909 postcard view was one of a series made to promote the building before it actually opened on 24 July 1909 and shows the 'public office'. On closer inspection it is possible to see that the light fittings are not quite complete, the window glass is still marked with whitewash for safety and there is a pile of builders' things tucked against the wall to the right.

The construction of Alfred Gelder Street required the demolition of many, often ancient, properties. This 1904 photograph was taken facing north along the original George Yard towards the old Town Hall, and shows demolition in progress. To the right of the picture is the George Yard Wesleyan Mission, shown just before it too was demolished in 1905. The present George Yard is situated to the east of its namesake.

Two
The New Town

The roof and frontage of the Punch public house are shown in this early view of one of Hull's lost streets, St John's Street. The former Willis's store, now the site of the Allder's department store, can also be seen centre-left. The buildings to the right were demolished for the construction of the City Hall and Victoria Square and the public toilets to the immediate left were demolished along with St John's church for the Ferens Art Gallery, c. 1925. St John's Street, named after the former church of St John's Myton, ran west from Monument Bridge to join Carr Lane at its junction with Waterhouse Lane and Engine Street. The entrance to Waterhouse Lane has been blocked off by the Princes Quay shopping centre and Engine Street was lost in the construction of the City Hall. As for St John's Street, all that remained to show its former location was a modern street sign that adorned a kerbside railing in Victoria Square until that too was recently removed.

The Corporation of the Trinity House funded the construction of this hospital and its associated buildings in 1834 on the south side of Carr Lane at the junction with Anne Street. Consequently the main feature of the central pediment was a carved representation of the hull of a ship. Rows of small almshouses were erected in 1848 to the rear and side of the hospital and some survived until 1958 although sadly the hospital had gone by that date. Following damage in the blitz it was demolished around 1943. (ML)

The Imperial Hotel opened in 1878 and was situated in Paragon Street on the site of the present Portland Hotel. Postcards were often used as advertising material and this card may well have been on sale at the hotel itself. The writer of the card was less than impressed with Hull, 'We do not think much of Hull and the Yorkshire people appear to be rather brusque'.

Following the Zeppelin bombing raids on Hull in 1916 there were many anti-German demonstrations, many of which ended in violence. Some families with German sounding names were attacked and the Hohenrien family, although they had long been respected in Hull, were persecuted to such an extent that they changed their name to Ross. This picture postcard from around 1905 shows one of their butchers' shops in Waterworks Street during happier times.

The McLoughlin family had been shoemakers in Hull since 1870. Originally at No. 5 Edward Street, they acquired Nos 2-4 West Street and from around 1905 expanded further to take in No. 1 Prospect Street. They remained in business at the same shop until the Second World War when many of the premises in the area were damaged during the blitz. Woolworth's now occupies the site of their shop, shown here at the corner of West Street and Prospect Street.

The Public Benefit Boot & Shoe Company was a national chain with many stores in Hull. Their Prospect Street store, shown here around 1906, was huge and lit by its own on-site gas engine. Situated at the corner of Prospect Street and Albion Street, the building became another victim of the blitz and was subsequently demolished. The main entrance of the Central Library now occupies the site.

Photographer William Parrish took this photograph in 1904 from outside the gates of the old Hull Royal Infirmary looking north along Prospect Street towards the Beverley Road junction. To the right are the stone walls of St Andrew's Presbyterian church of 1866. This too was lost in the blitz of 1941 and is now the location of the north side of the Central Library, at the corner of Baker Street.

In the year 2001 George Street is struggling to retain some of its fine terraces of Georgian and Victorian buildings. This 1903 winter scene shows what has already been lost. Many of the buildings on the left of the picture survive but the north side has suffered badly with the loss of the Grand Opera House, the frontage of the former Savings Bank, the Grand public house, the Dorchester cinema and many smaller shops and houses.

Paradise Row, also known as Carroll Place, may not be an address familiar to anyone but local historians and prospective newlyweds, as it is the location of Hull's Register Office. This busy looking cycle shop stood at the south-east corner of Paradise Row before it was foreshortened, when Charlotte Street was extended to meet the new North Bridge, in 1931. The Smithson family also ran a butcher's shop directly across the road, which no doubt had the best delivery cycles in the area. (KR)

Immediately to the east of the cycle emporium, house furnisher's Maw, Till, Kirke & Co. Ltd capitalised on the new road to the North Bridge and built their flagship store at the corner of the also shortened Trippett Street. All of their stores had closed by 1938 when the company was wound-up and now, minus its domes, the shop is home to a casino and part of the Hull City Archives.

Jameson Street was constructed between 1901-1903; the first section to be completed running from the north end of Savile Street through to King Edward Street. This view from around 1920 shows the street as a terminus for Holderness Road trams. All of the buildings shown were demolished during the 1950s and 1960s except three adjoining shops to the right, which survive as a building society and a camera shop.

Cattle travelling from the market in Commercial Road in the late 1890s. The buildings on the west side (left) of Savile Street, were lost for the construction of the first section of Jameson Street. During the 1960s the buildings in the centre of the picture in Bond Street and Smeaton Street were also lost for the creation of the present Bond Street dual carriageway. (ML)

Jameson Street and King Edward Street marked the beginning of Hull's new improved Edwardian city centre. Extravagant buildings were built throughout the city funded by Hull's success as a trading and manufacturing centre. A good example was the Prudential Building at the corner of Waterworks Street and King Edward Street shown to the left of this 1905 postcard view. The Prudential Insurance Company had provided a quarter of the funding required to build the first section of Jameson Street and King Edward Street.

Three
Everybody Likes a Parade

Charles Barraclough, an evangelist preacher from London, prepares to entertain the people of East Hull at the Holderness Road Presbyterian church. The church was built in 1874 in the Gothic Style and had seating for 1,100 people. Following blitz damage in 1941, services continued in the adjoining Sunday school. The church was demolished in 1972, but the former schoolroom survives, incorporated into the Green Man public house and bowling alley. Note the crouched children peering at the photographer from beneath the horse. Mr Barraclough appears to be the gentleman eighth from the left with bowler hat and bow tie.

The very popular Regatta Day, Victoria Pier, *c.* 1903. The almost dangerously large crowds were gathered to watch the equally dangerous sounding blindfold swimming race. Regattas had been held by the river, usually at the end of August, since 1829. They usually featured water-borne attractions but encouraged public participation too.

Indoor swimming is shown here at the opening of the Beverley Road Baths. Amongst the dignitaries at the official ceremony in 1905 was the father of the sender of this card. The message reads, 'puzzle – find Daddie and I'.

Sunday school demonstration, Hull, 1903. In the background can be seen the old Georgian housing in West Street and a glimpse of houses fronting Brook Street, prior to the extension of Jameson Street, and the construction of Hammond's store. The former B. Cooke's Kingston Observatory at the corner of Paragon Square, to the right of the picture, is the only building that survives from this time.

The previous parade passed along the same route as this funeral procession, seen here moving north along Brook Street, in 1903. It appears to have been the funeral of a postman, probably Edward Mitchell. The card was sent from No. 153 Clumber Street, the home of another postman John Mitchell, possibly a relative of the deceased, and reads, 'Dear Auntie, I am sending you this photo of poor dear Eddie's funeral'.

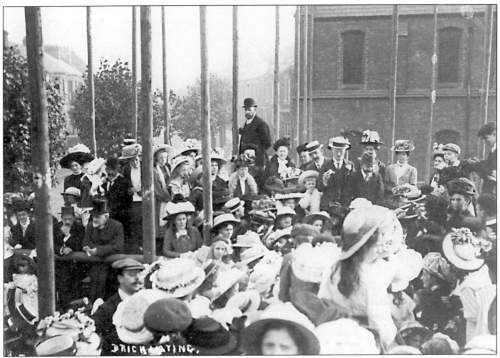

Photographer Arthur Seaman of Newstead Street took this crowded photograph of the bricklaying ceremony of the Plane Street Wesleyan Methodist church in 1910. Built to the designs of Gelder & Kitchen, the church is now closed and has been the target for continued vandalism in recent years.

A stone laying ceremony at the Prince's Avenue Wesleyan Sunday school attracted this small crowd on 3 April 1911. The crowd displays an amazing array of ladies' hats and men's moustaches.

A funeral was always guaranteed to attract a good crowd in the early years of the twentieth century. These locals brought the Botanic Railway Crossing on Spring Bank to a standstill on 27 October 1904 as the victims of the Dogger Bank trawler incident were taken to their graves in the Western Cemetery. The photograph, probably made from the top of a tram, shows the crowds even spilling on to the footbridge over the railway lines.

Another sombre occasion, a procession to mark the funeral of King Edward VII, 20 May 1910. The Hull police band marches in slow-time south along Prospect Street. The shops shown to the left were destroyed in the Second World War and are now the site of Woolworth's. The photograph was probably taken from the first floor window of the Wheatsheaf public house.

A happier occasion is recorded on this 1906 postcard which shows the winners of the 1st Prize for the best decorated 'car' from the Queens Hall Sunday School Union demonstration. The Queens Hall of 1905 was designed by architect Alfred Gelder and was situated in Alfred Gelder Street. Its grand entrance can be seen in the background of this photograph by John Osbourne of Norfolk Street.

Sunday hasn't always been the day when the family goes to the DIY stores! It was often the chance to go and see a parade or procession like this Military Sunday gathering on the old Corporation Field in Park Street. The pediment of the present Hull College in Park Street can be seen in the background of this photograph, which shows the first ever Military Sunday Parade held in Hull in June 1907.

Another Sunday, another parade. Members of the Kingston upon Hull & District Lodge of the National United Order of Free Gardeners Friendly Society prepare for a parade. The society was formed in 1866 but the view shown here, albeit undated, is probably around 1905.

GENERAL PASS TICKET

Admit the Bearer TO THE

RAILWAY STATION

& COVERED PART of THE PIER & ANGLES

on the Occasion of the Queens Visit,

viz ....

introduced by the Mayor. ....

Town Hall.

Hull, 9. October 1854

See other side

Sadly few photographs made during the visit of Queen Victoria to Hull on 9 October 1854 seem to have survived, although I do have a ticket to go! Amongst her duties on visiting Hull was the knighting of the mayor and a ceremonial tour of the town and its docks. Two triumphal arches were built along her route, one in Queen Street and another in Whitefriargate, a trend that continued for later Royal visits.

It is not a parade that is shown here, but an exhibition. Photographer Frank Overton was responsible for some of the views used in this book and was a typical photographer of his period (around 1904-14). A relative of Frank, who noted that it showed his first exhibition at this, his original address, No. 147 Beverley Road, sent this card 1905.

Four
Lost Churches and Chapels

Spring Bank, Hull. No.6.

The Church attracted more popular support in Edwardian Hull than it does today; Spring Bank alone had five churches and chapels which in total could seat 3,600 people with other chapels, only yards away in the side streets, seating thousands more. Church attendances were high during the earlier part of the twentieth century but there are few churches now left in the Spring Bank area. St Jude's Anglican church, on the south side of Spring Bank, was consecrated in 1874. Edward Simpson of Bradford designed the church in the Early English style and it had seating for 800. The fine building was demolished in the 1970s and a frozen food store and car park now fill the site. Just in the distance, on the right of the picture, can be seen the steeple of the former Swedenborgian church of 1875. The steeple is gone but the church survives.

This imposing building was the work of architects Gelder & Kitchen and was built in 1901 at a cost of £7,700. It was the chapel of the Newland Wesleyan School, and originally had seating for 850. A new church was built alongside in 1928. Situated at the corner of Newland Avenue and Cottingham Road it has subsequently been almost completely demolished and is the site of a car park.

Kings Hall Wesleyan Mission on the south side of Fountain Road replaced an earlier mission chapel that had been converted from a former Liberal Club. It is shown newly-built in this photograph of 1910 and had been designed by architects Gelder & Kitchen. Another victim of modern redevelopment, it had become out-dated by the time it was demolished in 1970. New housing now marks the site.

This well turned-out group was no doubt part of the congregation of the Zion Primitive Methodist chapel in Fountain Road; they are probably seated outside the slightly later Institute block of 1909. Both buildings were damaged during the blitz of the Second World War and demolished around 1960. The photograph was made by Edward Grocock, who lived nearby, at No. 72 Fountain Road.

The former Waltham Street Wesleyan chapel of around 1813 by William Jenkins had suffered during the blitz. However, as this slightly later photograph shows, it had only very minor damage and may well have been saved. In its heyday it held a congregation of 1,500 with ease but it had closed by 1932. Following its fall from grace the classically styled building was demolished in 1949.

Stepney Church, Hull.

Grand BAZAAR, Nov. 20, 21, and 22, 1907.

This pair of printed postcards (above and opposite) was used to advertize a bazaar that was held at the Stepney Methodist New Connexion chapel in November 1907. William Hill, a Leeds architect, designed the Gothic style building that was constructed in 1869 on the east side of Beverley Road.

Stepney Church, Hull.

Grand BAZAAR, Nov. 20, 21, and 22, 1907.

Situated just before the Bull Inn, the Stepney Chapel seated 600 and was built in 1849 to replace the smaller Zion Methodist New Connexion chapel across the road which ironically has outlived the chapel. Following its closure in 1966 it survived until around 1980 and a supermarket now occupies the site.

A surprising title to this photograph for what was obviously once a chapel. The marvellous crescent seating arrangement was an original feature of the former Humber Street Wesley chapel designed by William Sissons in 1832. It had seated 1,300 but was redundant by 1905 and became a saleroom for one of the many fruit companies in the area. It was severely damaged in the blitz during the Second World War and later demolished.

This grand brick built structure with stone dressings was situated at the corner of Bright Street and Holderness Road. Bright Street Primitive Methodist Connexion chapel was built in 1863-64 and had seating for around 1,200, but had seen its best days by the time of this postcard view of early 1904. It was damaged in the blitz of 1941 but went on to survive until around 1960.

St John the Evangelist Anglican church was the first church built outside the old town walls. It opened in 1792 as a chapel of ease to Holy Trinity and to serve the expanding new town particularly in the Myton area. This photograph from around 1910 shows the impressive interior before its demolition between 1917 and 1925 to make way for the Ferens Art Gallery. (KR)

Drypool, now another industrial suburb of Hull, was an ancient township far older than Hull itself. The earliest known record of a church in the village is from 1226 and other evidence suggests an even earlier building. St Peter's Anglican church shown in this photograph of around 1910 originates mainly from 1823 with later additions. It is seen here from the south side of the entrance to the Drypool Basin of the old Victoria Dock.

An unknown man standing in the porch of St Peter's in a picture postcard probably made by photographer William Mitchell of Mitchell & Cooper. Sadly, St Peter's was another victim of the blitz during the Second World War and it was almost completely destroyed with only the tower left standing. It was later demolished and the site is now a quiet garden in a busy commercial area.

Five
Scenes in Sculcoates

The construction of Hull's first dock in 1778 created a demand for land nearby and speculators were quick to capitalise on the new prosperity. Charles Street was one of many streets laid out in Georgian Hull in an area that was once gardens and farms. The street was laid out from around 1800 on land belonging to the Revd Charles Jarratt. Charles Street is shown here in the early 1930s, when it was the main shopping street for the local community. Most of the shops seen here in of the section between Wright Street and Francis Street, were household names in Hull – Maypole Dairy, Mallory's, Bromby's and the Argenta Meat Co. are all shown. The whole row was lost for the construction of Freetown Way in 1983. Only a very small section of original buildings survive in Charles Street, which ironically are some of the oldest. (ML)

The opposite side of the street to the previous image, with many more shops. This section between Alicia Street and Reform Street on the east side of Charles Street was lost, not to Freetown Way, but an earlier compulsory purchase scheme in 1938. Sadly, for the author, this included the demolition of his father's birthplace, a former family home and the birthplace of many of his relatives. (ML)

Charles Street joined Waterloo Street at the point where the Cottingham Drain crossed between the two, seen here in the early 1930s. This photograph shows the section of Waterloo Street between Richmond Terrace and the drain to the left of the picture, and Liddell Street to the right. A large open grassed area now occupies the site, which once included this author's birthplace at No. 33 Richmond Terrace. (ML)

Bethel Croft had seven shops around Hull between 1910 and 1940, and it is likely that this photograph was made following the opening of his new store at No. 14 Charles Street around 1910. The small shop in the oldest part of the street had once been home to a feather dyer's, but was perhaps best known as one of William Jackson's shops, of which there were three in Charles Street. The property was demolished in 1987 and replaced by modern flats.

Between the many shops and pubs in Waterloo Street were long terraces like this; Arthur's Terrace was one of many that ran east from Waterloo Street through to St Paul's Street. Running alongside the Crystal Hotel public house it ended opposite St Paul's church whose tower can be seen in the distance. The photograph was made as part of a record of air-raid shelter sites, one of which can be seen in the middle of this view around 1942. (HCA)

Compulsory purchase orders, issued from around 1967, eventually forced the demolition of almost all the buildings in this area of Sculcoates. Sadly that included this shop of pawnbroker and jeweller, Lazarus Levinson at the corner of Waterloo Street (No. 205) and Fountain Road (No. 91), seen here in 1915. (KR)

Fountain Road originally ran in a continuous line, crossing Waterloo Street on its route eastwards from Beverley Road to Wincolmlee. Thomas Wilford's house furnishing shop was situated at No. 128 Fountain Road, on the south side near to the Pacific Hotel, which was on the corner of St Paul's Street. It is shown here in a photograph of around 1914, probably soon after opening. The Wilfords remained at the same shop until the early 1930s, when Mrs Kate Wilford was listed as the keeper. (KG)

This unassuming building at No. 2a Sculcoates Lane; near to the Beverley Road junction, is passed daily by hundreds of cars. Most drivers will be unaware that this was one of the first motor garages and petrol stations which opened in Hull around 1914. It was originally owned by motor engineer Sydney Davidson. The small sign over the door of the garage indicates that the private address of the owner at the time of the photograph, was No. 6 Cromer Street St Leonard's Road. This suggests the photograph was made around 1920 when the garage had been taken over by Riseam & Co. also motor engineers. Mr William Riseam's home address was No. 6 Cromer Street.

Many of the residents of Alicia Street are gathered for a street photographer in this valued family photograph, c. 1925. The author's mother, father and many other relatives' are amongst the group at the eastern end of Alicia Street. Alicia Street was named after the daughter of

George Pryme on whose land it was built in around 1840. The alley shown to the rear of the photograph ran through to Caroline Street.

A moment in time from the late 1890s at the corner of Cave Street to the left, and Beverley Road. On the right is John Dobson's Park Hotel and in the distance can be seen the steeple of the Stepney Methodist New Connexion Chapel. Note the two distinct types of hired transport; a rather basic open topped fare-stage waggonette for the working gentlemen and a fine Hansom Cab for the more well-to-do. (ML)

Through the arched entry next to the Park Hotel was a beer-garden, which belonged to the hotel. Its rustic tables and benches are seen here with staff and regulars enjoying Moors' & Robson's beer around 1907. Small beer-gardens were common at that time and are not, as one might have assumed, a more recent invention.

The Sculcoates Union Workhouse, shown here in 1904, was first established in Beverley Road in 1844 and was designed by one of Hull's foremost architects Henry Francis Lockwood. To local people it was known more familiarly as the much-enlarged Kingston General Hospital, which has recently been demolished to make way for a new school.

Brunswick Avenue was laid out around 1880 and fully built upon by 1885. Strand Close, as Brunswick Avenue is now known, has only one building that survives from this 1905 postcard view. The building on the right, formerly the first of Hull's higher grade board schools, was known as Brunswick Avenue Junior High School when the author attended it in 1969. It is now used as a part of the city council's Social and Leisure Services offices.

An early motor car approaching the end of Terry Street as it proceeds north along Beverley Road in 1904. The message on this postcard reads, 'If you look on the other side you will see it is Doris & Nancy in the mail cart – Doris tells everybody she is going to America on a postcard'. Much of the terrace on the right of the picture survived until quite recently.

John Drury 'Builder & Contractor, Bricklayer & Plasterer, Dealer in all kinds of Building Materials etc.', lived at No. 52 Brunswick Avenue, but his business address was Langdale Buildings on the west side of Beverley Road. The elaborate yard and buildings were almost opposite the end of Brunswick Avenue. As this 1897 billhead shows, he also had another family member carrying on an undertaker's business from his premises.

Six

Spring Bank and the Avenues

Spring Bank originated as a narrow lane, which ran alongside the old Spring Dyke, an early source of fresh water for the town from Springhead. The Lime trees, which lined the centre of Spring Bank, marked the route of the Dyke and survived until the mid-1920s by which time they had become an obstruction to modern vehicles. Dominating this animated Spring Bank scene of around 1905 is the former Jubilee Primitive Methodist chapel of 1864, to the right of the picture. Situated at the corner of Freehold Street, the Italianate masterpiece was replaced by the present St Stephen's Anglican church in 1959, in typical bland post-war style. It is unlikely that Spring Bank will ever regain its former status as a grand boulevard, but efforts are currently being made to improve its appearance, which has been neglected of late.

No matter what the Season, friend,
No matter what the weather,
You'll always spend your money well,
You and the Coults together.

Published by G. M. Coult, 133, Spring Bank, Hull.

Newsagent George Martin Coult is shown here at the door of his shop at No. 133 Spring Bank. His window is filled with picture postcards of the type used to illustrate this book. He acted as a publisher and postcard agent for many local photographers and ran his business from around 1905 until at least 1943. His old shop survives and is still a newsagent's today, almost a hundred years later.

Next door but one, to the west of Coult's shop, was family butcher Fred Steele at No. 137 Spring Bank. The message on the reverse noted, 'I have sent you this photo of Cyril, he is the little one with one hand in his pocket.' Photographer Frank Overton, whose agent was George Coult, made this photographic postcard in around 1904.

I think the 1860s frontages of these houses in Sydenham Villas may well have been unique in Hull. This image of around 1904 shows children from the area posing for photographer, Frank Overton. Sydenham Villas ran alongside St Jude's church, and was the first terrace off the east side of Stanley Street, Spring Bank.

On the north side of Spring Bank, opposite Stanley Street, is Middleton Street, at the bottom of which was the former Middleton Street Board School. Although it closed as a school in 1941 the building still survives, although semi-derelict, after many changes of use. One doubts it will ever see a group of school children like this again pictured here in about 1905. (ML)

Sadly the former Botanic Newsagency and Vaughan's piano shop no longer grace the north-west corner of Spring Bank. They are shown here, amid some marvellous advertising in a photograph from around 1918, possibly decorated in celebration of the end of the First World War. The premises are now a vividly coloured print-shop.

All of these buildings, including the central lodge, probably of around 1852, belonged to the Hull General Cemetery Co. whose cemetery was situated directly behind them. The cemetery is now a popular walking area but tragically the buildings were demolished just after this photograph was taken in 1907, when Prince's Avenue was widened at this point.

As the south end of Prince's Avenue gradually became the local shopping area it was inevitable that the Hull Co-operative Society Ltd would choose this location for a new branch. Their fine store at No. 73 Prince's Avenue still survives in another guise at the corner of Clumber Street, but the window displays are less elaborate today.

At first glance this view looking north along Prince's Avenue in around 1905 appears quite ordinary. Look closer and you will see it shows all of the property on the east side as private houses. Today, they are either shops or in some cases demolished for more modern buildings including a public house. The Fish Street Memorial church at the corner of Duesberry Street gives a guide to the location.

Blenheim Street, another of the long streets running off the west side of Prince's Avenue, is shown here in the winter of 1904. Local photographer Arthur Seaman of Newstead Street took this photograph. No parked cars in sight, just a milk-cart!

This section of Chanterlands Avenue was almost completely built upon by 1919, mostly by private housing with a few solitary shops. This view looking north from the junction with Perth Street in around 1929 shows a variety of delivery vehicles calling at shops in the avenue.

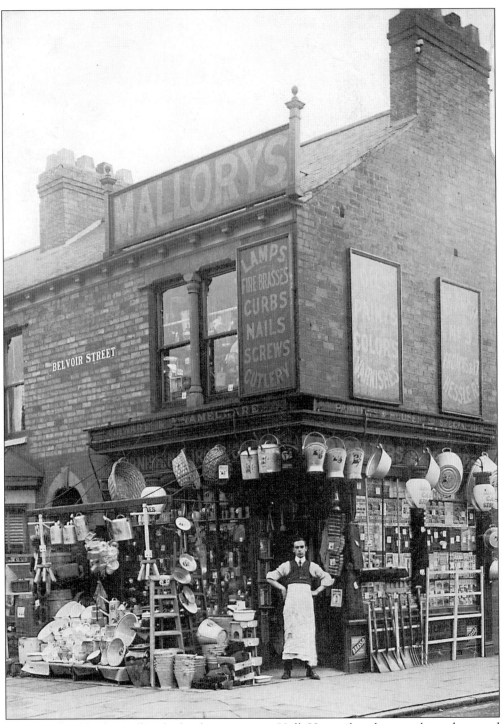

In 1892 John Charles Mallory had only one store in Hull. He was listed as an oil merchant and drysalter at No. 11 Hessle Road in a trade directory of that year. By the time of this picture of his Belvoir Street store in around 1910, on the corner of Hardwick Street, Mallory's had expanded its empire to sixteen stores in Hull. (KG)

Number 222 Park Avenue, Southfield, as this house was named, was home to the family of Henry Booth the founder of the Hull printing company of that name. This postcard view was sent as a Christmas greeting card from Mr and Mrs Booth on 24 December 1913. The house at the corner of Richmond Street was demolished in 1984 but has been replaced by a sympathetically designed building used as flats.

The former Victoria Avenue Fountain, now another of the avenues' lost fountains, c. 1905. This charming view, with a half-built Salisbury Street in the background includes what appears to be a postboy and his friends gathering for a chat as they pose at the junction of Salisbury Street and Victoria Avenue.

Children in Ella Street photographed by William Parrish. The street has remained largely unchanged although the lines of cast-iron railings were sadly taken in error for the war-effort and were never replaced.

Reynoldson Street was probably less well-to-do than Ella Street in the Edwardian era and the quality of housing shown in this 1904 photograph reflects this. The children are huddled around what appears to be a photographer's hand-cart, probably belonging to the photographer, W.S. Parrish of Parrish & Berry Ltd.

We will never know why the children gathered around the window of the Mallory's store at the corner of Newland Avenue and Lambert Street. Perhaps it was a chilly morning and the store provided heat. To the left of this 1904 photograph can be seen the sign of the former Yorkshire Laundries premises on the corner of Sharp Street.

No selection of photographs of the Avenues' district would be complete without a photograph made in Pearson Park. This wintry scene from 1904 was one of a series made by Parrish & Berry and used as Christmas greetings cards. The same group of girls was taken at a variety locations in the park posing 'naturally' for the camera.

Walter Edward Cullen, a former painter and signwriter, may well have painted the signs over his new shop himself. The Falmouth Street post office at the corner of Cottingham Road and Falmouth Street was probably newly built in this photograph of around 1910. Falmouth Street had only just been completed by this date.

Seven
West of the City

Fried fish and fried chips originated in this country, in different areas during the 1840s, but came together as the 'Fish & Chip' shop in the 1850s. Dickens referred to a 'fried fish warehouse' in *Oliver Twist* in 1839. The first known fish and chip shop in the north of England, was allegedly in Mossely Lancashire, in 1863. In Hull, shops began to appear from around 1880 specifically as fried fish dealers, many of the owners having previously been in related trades. Miss Elsie Wilson stands at the door of her parents' fish shop at No. 78 Londesborough Street in this postcard, which was sent 28 December 1908. She included 'best wishes for a prosperous New Year', in the message that was sent to friends in Barton upon Humber. This shop and all of the other property on the north side of the street has been lost to modern housing developments.

One of the many streets, which were demolished on the north side of Londesborough Street, was Wyndham Street. This view from around 1905 looks east along the street towards Wenlock Street in the distance. A coalman and a grocer can be seen delivering door to door from their carts. Note the complete absence of any other sort of vehicle.

Looming out of the mist at the rear of the former Western General Hospital is its replacement, the present Hull Royal Infirmary, c. 1965. These charming old buildings (originally the Hull Workhouse of 1852) were demolished to make a forecourt for the new fourteen-storey building, which was completed in 1966. (HCA)

Two Anlaby Road trams pass one another on the east side of the old Anlaby Road railway level crossing, *c*. 1912. The crossing was replaced in 1965 by the present flyover bridge. The two largest buildings in the picture survive today; St Matthew's church and to its right the former Boulevard Higher Grade School.

Boulevard Higher Grade School was the third of Hull's higher grade schools to be built. Opening in 1895 it closed almost a hundred years later in 1988 and is now used as flats re-named Rosedale Mansions. It is shown here in a busy scene from 1904 with a delivery cart from Soulsby & Wood of Blackfriargate ambling south along the street.

Coltman Street has fallen from grace somewhat in recent years and has its share of modern inner-city problems. However, at the time of this 1904 photograph, it was at the height of its popularity and was home to some very well-to-do inhabitants. To the left are some of the first properties to be erected in the street, dating from around 1840, and built in the Greek Revival style. Parked cars would prevent this photograph from being repeated today.

Slightly less grand than Coltman Street, Gordon Street (originally Fitzroy Street) was part of a development of streets by the Strickland-Constable family in the Boulevard area. The old council school, one of a fine selection of original buildings in the street, can be seen to the left of the picture with the Boulevard in the distance.

Hawthorn Avenue was mainly a residential street, interspersed with several shopping areas, and William Henry Pattison was a well-known butcher at No. 53 for many years. The casual alfesco manner in which his meat is displayed would today, no doubt, incur the wrath of the environmental health department.

A gleaming Dairycoates tram passes a horse-drawn Hessle Road fare-stage waggonette in this 1904 view. It shows the junction of Hessle Road and St Georges Road with Gillett Street running off to the right. Traffic lights now control the junction and the former Wesleyan chapel on the left, demolished in the late 1960s, has recently been replaced by a shoe shop.

The Hull Brewery Co. Ltd had many outlets in and around Hull for the sale of their beers, wares, wine and spirits for consumption off the premises. The off-licence is still a familiar type of shop around Hull but few will have a display to match the 1930s shop of William Elkington at No. 928 Hessle Road on the corner of St Nicholas Avenue.

Hull's livestock market had been situated in the Market Place, Fish Street and latterly Waterhouse Lane where it had been since 1782. In 1818 that site was sold to the Dock Co. for the construction of Junction Dock and in 1838 it moved to this purpose-built site in Edward's Place, Commercial Road. In the distance can be seen the Railway Dock, and centre-left the old Whittington Inn, before its re-front of around 1900. The Cattle Market was demolished in the late 1980s and is now the site of a retail park. (KR)

Eight
A Night on the Town

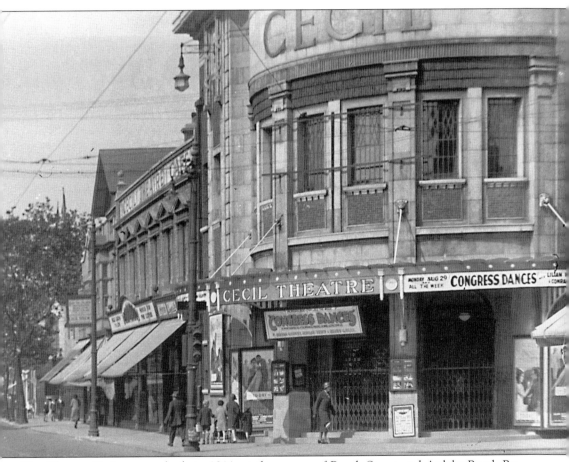

The Theatre De Luxe was built in 1911, at the corner of Brook Street and Anlaby Road. By 1925 it had become known as the Cecil Theatre, as it is shown here around 1933. The impressive Art Deco building was badly damaged during an incendiary attack in the Second World War and stood as a shell for many years. The southern extension of Ferensway, beyond Anlaby Road, required the demolition of many properties, including the former theatre, which was demolished in 1953. Its site is now marked by the bronze glass structure of Europa House of 1974, diagonally opposite the later Cecil of 1955 that was built to replace it. The roof of the surviving College of Art can be seen to the left of the cinema. (CJK)

On the left of this view is the stylish arched entrance of the former Kinemacolour Palace, which opened in 1910 and is seen here around 1915. It was built in only seven weeks and by 1919 had changed its name to become the Regent Cinema. The Regent is now a popular public house, but in recent years has been redeveloped at the rear to provide car-parking facilities.

The gleaming Art Deco frontage of the Rialto Cinema can be seen to the left beyond a brick-built public convenience at the entrance to Terry Street, Beverley Road, in 1933. Built as the Coliseum in 1912, on part of a former skating rink, it became the Rialto in the 1920s. Following the closure of the nearby National Cinema, during the Second World War, the Rialto took over its name. It closed as a cinema in 1961 and later became a bowling alley until it was destroyed by fire in 1974.

This postcard was produced by the Kingston Varieties Co. to promote the opening of the Tivoli Theatre in 1912. The Tivoli was created from the former Theatre Royal, which had originally opened in 1846, at the corner of Paragon Street and South Street. The Tivoli was an immensely popular venue that was sadly missed following its closure and untimely demolition in 1957.

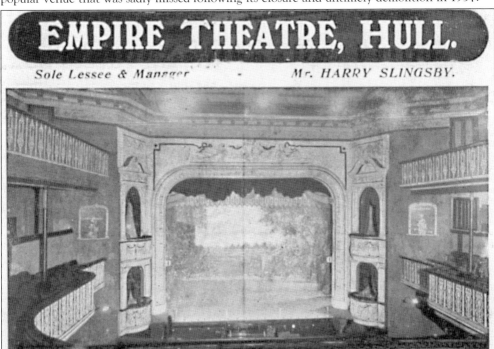

An advertising card, showing the interior of the Empire Theatre, c. 1902. The Empire, a music hall, stood at the corner of George Street and Grimston Street and was more famously known in Hull as the Criterion Cinema, with two ceramic lions guarding the entrance and steps. It closed in 1973 and was demolished and later replaced by the Comet Group building.

Seen here in the 1930s the former Eureka Picture Palace is another local landmark building fondly regarded by the tight-knit community of Hessle Road. It opened its doors in 1912 but ceased showing films in 1959. It has since declined steadily and the building is currently merely a shell, threatened with imminent demolition. (HCA)

The former Waterloo Picture House in Waterloo Street was licensed as a cinema from 1920. It is seen here in the late 1970s as a deserted Bingo hall. It had ceased showing films in 1959 but remained a popular club and social venue for the residents of the Waterloo Street area until its closure in 1977. It was demolished in 1980. (KR)

The canopy over the entrance to the Central Picture Theatre can be seen at the extreme left of this 1933 photograph of Prospect Street. To its right is the entrance to the Hole in the Wall public house and in the distance are the sorely missed buildings of Blundell's Corner. (CJK)

The Central Picture Theatre was the smallest cinema in the city centre and opened in 1916 as the Prospect Picture House. It seated only 1,000 but had a very chic café, complete with grand piano, shown in this interior photograph around 1920. This cosy cinema was destroyed during the blitz of 1941 and is now the site of an office block.

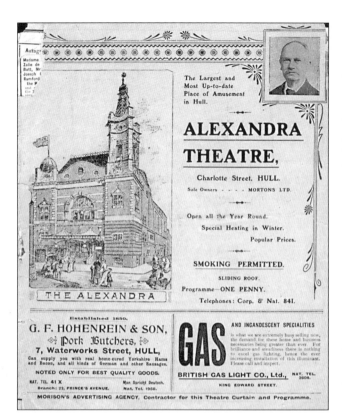

If you visited the theatre you had to have a programme and this Alexandra Theatre programme from 1906 is filled with local advertisements but very little about the programme on offer. The Alexandra was situated in Charlotte Street and opened on 13 December 1902. Its tower was a Hull landmark and could be seen for miles over the rooftops. By 1907 it was also in use as an early cinema, showing films using the Vitograph system. Still popular in the late 1930s it had two variety shows each night (6.40 p.m. and 8.50 p.m.) seven days a week. Sadly, even if it had not been demolished following blitz damage it would no doubt have been lost for the construction of Freetown Way, which would have run straight across its entrance hall.

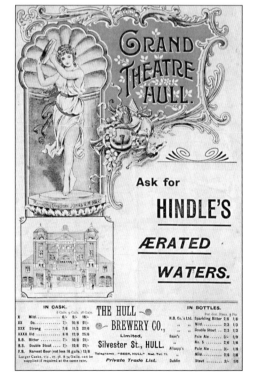

Another lively theatre programme cover (in full colour) for the Grand Opera House in George Street from 1899. Note the prices of the beer in the Hull Brewery advertisement at the foot of the page. George Street had many theatres and cinemas, over the years, including the Grand Opera House and Theatre. The theatre was built in 1893 at a cost of £20,000 and by 1930 was showing films as the Grand Theatre Cinema. In 1935 it closed for refurbishment and re-opened as the Dorchester Cinema, which it remained until its closure in 1977. Following demolition in 1987 the site was redeveloped as a bar adjoined by a number of shops. (see also p. 27).

Nine

East of the River

The Groves is an ancient part of Hull, consisting largely of the area between Lime Street and New Cleveland Street. The thousands of people who lived there worked in industries on both sides of the river, commuting by small ferryboats and later over bridges. This tight-knit community has now all but disappeared. Historically the old road from Hull to the village of Sutton ran along the route of Lime Street and on through Stoneferry Road until the construction of a more direct route, New Cleveland Street. The new street, ran south to Witham from the junction shown here; Jenning Street on the left and St Mark's Street to the right. The new road provided a more accessible route for modern industrial traffic. Raine's Groves Sheet Metal Works is shown here around 1905. The housing in the area was mostly demolished in slum clearances during the 1930s.

Not a single building shown in this fascinating photograph of Spyvee Street in 1907 by Hull photographers Parrish & Berry Ltd survives today. The whole of the street, which runs east from New Cleveland Street was formerly used as a ropewalk – hence its length and straightness. It is now given over to retail and industrial premises.

These buildings were the General Office (centre) and Kingston Works (far left) of Reckitt & Sons Ltd in Dansom Lane. On the right can be seen the former Bird in Hand beer house, which closed on 2 June 1923 when it was sold to Reckitt's for £7,500 by owners Hewitt's of Grimsby. Soon after it was demolished for expansion of their works.

Another view of the same office building, but this time from the corner of Kent Street on the opposite side of Dansom Lane. Kent Street is now one of Hull's lost streets. It originally ran south all the way through to the Holderness Road.

All of the properties in Witham shown in this photograph were demolished around 1929 to make way for the new North Bridge scheme. Photographed from the entrance to Great Union Street the terrace included the Kings Arms (built around 1805) which was re-built near the new bridge in 1928 by George Houlton & Sons on behalf of Moors' & Robson's Ltd.

Here at the door of his shop at No. 130 Witham is George Rumsby who was a corn dealer from the 1870s until the 1920s. His shop was situated in the small section of Witham, often known as Bridge-foot, which led to the old North Bridge. The shop and all of the neighbouring properties, including the North Bridge Hotel, were demolished following blitz damage .

Once a common site on Hull's streets, these ornate cast iron urinals were phased out from the early 1930s when they were either replaced by brick structures, or more often, not replaced at all. Only one cast iron example survives in this area, situated in New Walk, Beverley; many of the other brick versions are currently being demolished. (CJK)

This 1904 view shows the former Drypool Green to the left and the junction of Hedon Road to the right. The Commercial Inn (centre) and the factories on the banks of the River Hull were all demolished following bomb damage in the Second World War. None of the buildings shown here survive today.

John Tebb 'dispensing chemist, druggist, & seedsman' had been in Hull since at least 1879 when he had a shop in Newington, Hessle Road. His later, and much larger premises, included this shop at No. 46 Beaumont Street, Drypool, seen here around 1900. The business carried on trading from the same address into the 1950s. (RT)

This unlikely business union of shipping contractor and butcher was begun by John Dineley, c. 1910. The splendid shops were situated at Nos 303-305 Hedon Road opposite the old Alexandra Dock entrance. The property is now the site of a motorcycle shop.

The open-topped tram on its return journey from Marfleet is just passing the Hull Prison and yard of monumental sculptor George Henry Leake on the corner of Southcoates Avenue. To the left of his yard, in this photograph of 1906, workmen are busy preparing to erect telegraph poles near a vacant plot of land. The site is now occupied by Newtown Buildings, which were constructed in around 1930.

A busy scene at the corner of Marfleet Lane and Hedon Road in the early 1930s. Most of these buildings have recently been demolished to make space for a roundabout as part of the new dual carriageway plans for Hedon Road. Sadly this also required the demolition of the New Inn, shown here to the right of the tram.

W.J. Fletcher, hairdresser turned photographer and member of the Hull Photographic Society, took this photograph in around 1910. It shows the greengrocer's shop of Joseph Emerson at No. 70 Newbridge Road. It may have been made as a Christmas greeting card, as bunches of holly and small Christmas trees can be seen hanging over the window and door.

A once familiar sight on Hull's streets were police call boxes. This was Hull City police call box No. 11 and it was situated at the north end of Southcoates Lane at the junction with Holderness Road. The building in the background was the former Trustee Savings Bank, which is now used as a public house.

The message on the rear of this postcard, sent in 1910 reads, 'Dear Mabel, I am sending you a view of your Uncle Frank's shop. Winnie will be able to tell you all about it'. The shop in question was the second from the left in this row of four; Frank Mundey, whose grocery was situated opposite the East Park on the corner of Telford Street and Holderness Road.

The hand-cart on the left of this 1904 view may well have been that of the photographer William Parrish. The children of Morrill Street guarded it for him as he took one of the many hundreds of images his company made of Hull during the Edwardian era.

Another Parrish & Berry photograph, but this time of the Holderness Road. Bright Street is on the left, now merely a works entrance, and the Liberal Club, to the far right, is also long gone. The Holderness Road baths and James Reckitt library on the right have both so far survived the ravages of war and redevelopment.

RECKITT'S GARDEN VILLAGE
from the Air

This aerial photograph shows the whole of Reckitt's Garden Village, probably photographed in the early 1930s as there appears to be no sign of Chamberlain Road which was constructed in that decade.

Ten
Work Hard

Although full employment today seems like an impossibility, it was not always so. This chapter takes a look at some of the people of Hull, at their various places of work, and in and out of uniform. It is pleasing to see most of these workers smiling for the camera. An almost entirely female group of workers from the flour mills of Joseph Rank & Sons are gathered here together outside the Clarence Street factory around 1917. This was the height of the First World War and therefore most of the men would have been away fighting in the trenches. During the Second World War the fighting came closer to home as this mill and associated buildings were extensively damaged during the blitz.

The message on the back of this postcard reads, 'Here is another one for your collection – Hetty Whitehouse on the wards'. The wards in question were those of the former Hull Royal Infirmary in Prospect Street. The postcard was produced by local photographer Victor Brearley, of nearby Norfolk Street, and posted by Hetty in 1905.

The former Blue Bell in Waterworks Street was re-named the Albany Hotel around 1900. The ornate bar and shelves in this photograph of around 1926 show the bar staff when the Albany was a Higson's Brewery house. All of the north side of Waterworks Street was demolished after the Second World War for the Queens House development.

The building which serves as the backdrop for this postcard view was the Sculcoates police station near the junction with Swann Street, c. 1921. It was built around 1878 as the headquarters of the 'C' Division. The men grouped beneath the huge gaslamp that marked the entrance was probably the whole of 'C' Division.

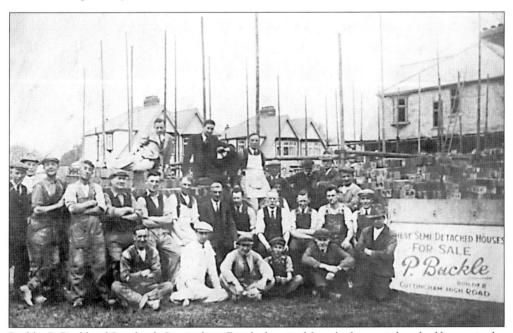

Builder P. Buckle of Overland, Cottingham Road advertised for sale the semi-detached houses in the background of this photograph, c. 1940. The stylish houses were very likely to have been the last of the houses to be built in Hall Road. They were also probably amongst the last quality houses to be built until after the Second World War and the post-war shortage of building materials.

This is the White Lion public house in the course of construction by builders Fenner, Panton & Co. Ltd, 10 May 1934. Ironically this pub is currently under threat of demolition to make way for a new shopping development. To the rear of the view new office blocks in Ferensway are advertised to let.

Only one half-smiling face is apparent amongst these Probationers within the walls of Hull Prison in 1908. The ironic message on the card says, 'excuse the smiles but we had been feeding off vinegar so didn't feel sweet, Au-revoir, Jim.'

A stonemason with a hammer in hand and a colleague with a pair of binoculars scan the skies over Hull in 1907 after adding the final touches to the statuary on the New Town Hall, more familiarly known to us today as the Guildhall. The sculpture in view, often mistaken for Bodecia, is called Maritime Prowess by A.H. Hodge, depicting a female figure at the prow of a boat drawn by seahorses. (KR)

Close inspection of this photograph reveals that the members of the Hull & Barnsley Railway Police-Ambulance Division, of Alexandra Dock, have been sitting in the pouring rain waiting for this photograph to be taken. They appear to have won a series of impressive looking awards.

Storry, Smithson & Co. Ltd were listed in a trade directory of 1929 as 'paint, colour, and varnish: oil boilers and refiners'. The members of staff from the Bankside works are shown here in 1927. The signboard reads 'Wolves 0 City 2 – a likely story!

Fish filleters on Billingsgate, Hull in 1904. The message on the reverse of this card noted, 'all alive oh! Haddock 7 for 6d, Plaice 14 for 6d this morning.' Billingsgate was an area on the north side of St Andrews Dock opposite the Riverside Quay.

This is a sight no longer to be seen in Hull, as our fruit now comes in container lorries, direct from the Roll-on Roll-off ferries at King George Dock. Taken by Wellsted & Son in 1910 and entitled Fruit Market Promenade, this photograph shows one of the huge transit sheds that were formerly around the old Humber Dock.

This unusual photograph was probably taken to be used as an advertisement for Rayment &
Sharpe, ship's stores, dealers and sail and cover makers, of Nos 158-159 High Street. The
business was established around 1872 and nearly ruined by fire in 1907. This view probably
shows a temporary works in High Street, which continued to trade until the early 1930s.

A sunny morning in High Street in 1933 with workmen in their waistcoats re-laying the
worn road surface, apparently using wooden sets. To the right is the Wilberforce House
museum and in the distance the still complete terraces of Georgian houses. These were
almost completely demolished following blitz damage. Only two now remain and are used as
part of the museum complex.

This 1906 postcard view shows the workmen of building contractor George H. Panton on the scaffolding around the partially completed City Hall. The lengthy construction period caused uproar at the time, when many new streets and dozens of new buildings were all being built simultaneously, bringing chaos and huge amounts of dust and dirt to the city. The corner of Engine Street can be seen to the left of the scaffolding.

Carts and rullys used by commercial businesses gradually gave way to motorized vehicles in the early part of the twentieth century. This early lorry belonged to the General Electric Welding Co. and although the company offices were in Charlotte Street they had works entrances in Dock Street. The vehicle is shown in a Dock Street yard near to the former Queens Dock entrance.

This unusual group photograph shows North Eastern Railway Co. staff on the platform at Paragon Station all holding copies of *Hull Topics*, a local advertising paper. The cover shows cinema advertisements including one for the Kinema Picture Palace that dates the photograph to around 1915.

Eleven

Play Hard

The delivery vehicles of Riley's Dairies Ltd were once a familiar sight on the streets of Hull. As well as their dairy and commercial fleet, Riley's also had a subsidiary company known as Grey Cars Ltd and, like many local firms, Riley's took their staff on outings in large vehicles often referred to as charabancs. The Grey Cars vehicle in this view from around 1930 was a solid-wheeled Albion, registration AT 4816, first registered in 1920. The Albion was originally made to seat twenty-nine, and must have been full to capacity, as the outing set off from outside Riley's Campbell Street works. The smart chap at the front wearing a flat cap was Mr Riley himself.

John Braithwaite, a haulage contractor of No. 2 Lime Tree Villas Sutton, loaned his vehicle for the purposes of entering a Commonwealth Day parade in the early 1930s. The photograph shows a bevy of girls in costume on board in the yards of the Londesborough Street barracks prior to the parade.

A chapter on Hull's social life would be incomplete without at least one Hull Fair photograph. Here is one from 1904 which shows that little has changed except the fashions, the prices and, I suspect, the noise level.

If you couldn't get to the fair, or more likely couldn't afford it, then why not make your own entertainment? This open-air street party took place in one of the many terraces off Scarborough Street. The occasion is not known (possibly a peace tea?) but from personal experience I recall as a child we had street parties every summer, just because it was summer!

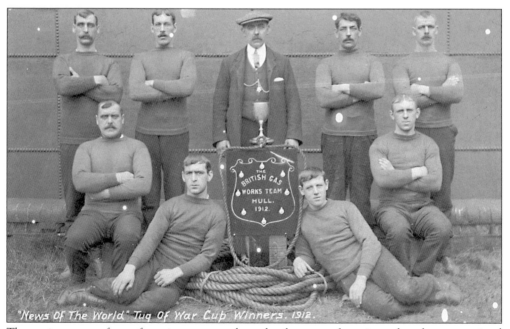

The ancient sport of tug-of-war is not as popular today, but many factories and works teams existed before the Second World War, when other forms of entertainment was limited. The British Gas, Bankside Works, tug-of-war team, seen here in 1912 alongside one of the company's gasometers, was obviously successful. They were the proud owners of the *News of the World* cup for that year.

JOY IN EAST

The location and occasion for this photograph are a mystery. Entitled by the photographer 'Joy in East Hull', it has been suggested that it was a Glee Meeting – the crowd with arms raised certainly appear happy! The predominantly working class crowd was gathered in an area that

appears to be piled high with railway sleepers and may have been in the Abbey Street area, near the former Southcoates railway station.

Football has long been a popular pastime for the masses and early games often descended into violence. This prison team from 1908 looks fairly fierce but it's hard to know whether it is the staff or the inmates who are posing for the camera!

Needlers AFC team appears younger and a less intimidating team than that of the prison! Seen here in 1912 they were one of many sports and social groups that the benevolent Fred Needler organised for his workers. The Needler's factory in Sculcoates Lane had its own sports field and cricket pavilion in later years. A happy workforce was a productive one. Most of those in the photograph spent their entire working lives with the company.

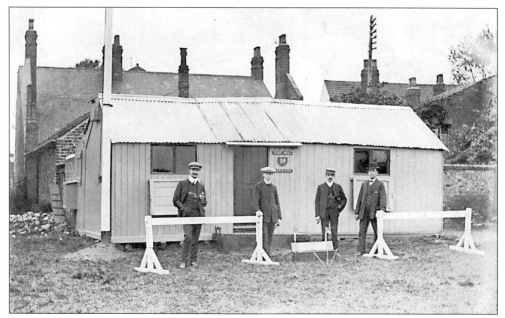

Hull had many Harrier cross-country running clubs, many formed when the sport was at its peak in the late 1880s. Clubs included the Stepney Harriers, the YPI Harriers, the Boulevard Harriers, and even the Hull Shop Assistants Harriers. Members of the East Hull Harriers are seen here, pipes in hand, probably at the rear of the Four In Hand pub on the Holderness Road from where they often raced.

The American Roller Rink, known officially as the Palladium Roller Rink, brought the American hobby to the notice of the Hull public around 1910. All the fancy-dress contestants are on skates in the Main Hall, which was also home to the Coliseum Cinema. The skating rink closed in 1914 to be replaced by a snooker hall.

Snappily dressed members of the Kingston Bowling & Social Club are shown here enjoying a peaceful game at their popular club in 1910. The club and green were situated to the rear of property in Ash Grove, Beverley Road and had just opened when the photograph was taken.

As well as an impressive bowling-green surface, the club had a superb pavilion complete with this well fitted-out smoke room for the members. The Queens Bowling Club at the Queens public house, Queens Road, had been formed much earlier; the Kingston Club may have been a response to the growing popularity of the game in the area.

The Hull United Liberal Club snooker team played their home matches from a club just to the west of the Holderness Road Baths and James Reckitt library. These rather austere looking gentlemen of the club, seen here around 1908, had just won a victory over Pearson's Institute in nearby Cleveland Street and, according to their notice board, were 'in the pink'.

This huge crowd of children have gathered at the front of a social club at Nos 28-29 Pryme Street, at its junction with Russell Street, c. 1930. The club had been formed from two private houses around 1900 and was later home to the Irish National Club from around 1905. Renamed the Russell Club in the late 1920s, it became the Central School of Dancing in the 1930s, known locally as Madame Sylvia's. The building was demolished around 1969.

A happy group of children photographed in 1926 by portrait photographer William Duncan of Anlaby Road. The Middleton Street Girls School choir had just won the 'tonic sol fa test', sight reading, at the Hull Music Festival.

The Hull Ice House Band was a Salvation Army brass band, 1922. They were formed from members of the Hull Ice House Citadel (2nd Corps) based at Anlaby Road under the Field Major and Mrs Walsh. The building used by Ice House Citadel still survives near Midland Street, but is no longer used by the Salvation Army. The present Ice House Citadel is based in nearby Adelaide Street.

Another starting point for outings was often the local pub. The ladies and gentlemen of the Cricketer's Arms public house in Prospect Street are seen here around 1930 outside the marvellous tiled frontage of the building (c. 1910). Situated at No. 86 Prospect Street, near the Baker Street junction, the building was badly damaged in the Second World War and later demolished.

A smaller group, all male this time, seated outside the Carpenter's Arms beer-house in Great Union Street. Most likely a sports team (darts?) they were dressed in their Sunday best with landlord William Stamp sitting proudly centre-front. The pub was redundant by 1937 and closed only to be bombed in 1941.

Some of these men gathered outside the Victoria Dock Tavern look as though they have enjoyed a life on the seas. The pub survives as popular as ever in Great Union Street. It has been a licensed premises from at least 1830 and is seen here in a photograph from around 1905.

It is only fitting to end a chapter on play with those masters of the art, children. The children in question in this candid 1904 photograph were at play in the children's corner of West Park. The photograph was made for a picture postcard and was sent by the photographer himself, William Parrish, to a friend in Newbald. The message reads, 'How do you think Newbald Green would look if it had a few of these attractions?' (KR)

Twelve
The River Hull
and the Docks

Stoneferry, now a predominantly industrial area, was once a thriving village and its trading history can be traced to the sixteenth century. Until relatively recently it retained many of its older buildings and as a point of transhipment and a convenient crossing point over the river Hull its importance is still felt today. This view, taken around 1950, looking south towards Hull shows the old Hewetson's Oil Mill, recorded as early as 1823, but probably much older. The miller's house, just visible to the right of the mill complex, has eighteenth-century architectural details. In the foreground two chaps navigate the river at one of the sites of the old stone-ferry. (ML)

The old Stoneferry Bridge is shown here in a postcard sent in November 1905, just a month after the bridge had opened. In the background, the chimneys of the former Stoneferry waterworks tower over the few buildings in the area.

The Sculcoates Bridge and Swann Street, c. 1935. The bridge was constructed in 1875, and provided two-way access for the many workers who travelled from their homes in the Groves to the Sculcoates mills and factories, and those who made the opposite journey east from their homes to work in the Groves and Wilmington districts. Only the bridge now remains from this view. (KR)

This photograph was featured in the souvenir programme for the opening of the new North Bridge on Monday 10 August 1931. The old, horizontal drawbridge of 1870 had served the city well and was replaced by the present Scherzer bascule bridge. The estimated total cost for the whole of the works was £258,500, and as the picture shows, the old bridge remained in service whilst the new one was constructed and tested.

Salthouse Lane Bridge opened in 1888 and was the template for the later Stoneferry Bridge. Compare the two and you will see very little difference. Originally linking Salthouse Lane (Alfred Gelder Street from around 1902) and Clarence Street, the bridge had become too narrow for modern traffic by the 1950s and was replaced by the present Drypool Bridge in 1958. The new bridge retains a decorative plaque from the old.

The Drypool Basin of the Victoria Dock seen from the entrance to the dock from the Old Harbour in the River Hull, *c*. 1915. St Peter's church can be seen to the left of the photograph and had overlooked the dock since its construction in 1850.

The Hull & Barnsley Railway's Alexandra Dock opened in 1885 and remains one of Hull's busiest to this day. In this 1904 photograph showing goods being unloaded from a vessel in the dock, the workers appear to be wearing a sort of uniform. The cases, shown sliding down wooden skids, were laboriously loaded by hand onto trains or carts for onward despatch.

Alexandra Dock's largest and most frequent incoming cargo was and still is timber. Hull imports over a million cubic metres of softwoods each year, mostly from Russia, Scandinavia and the Baltic States. This 1930s aerial view shows Alexandra Dock and the Alexandra Dock extension covered in timber from end to end.

Queen's Dock, *c.* 1910. Many local people will be aware that the present Queen's Gardens resulted from the filling in, during the early 1930s, of the former Queen's Dock of 1778. It is now hard to imagine scenes like this in the very heart of the city centre. The view faces east and the present Guildhall Road is on the right of the picture.

Prince's Dock, the site of the modern Princes Quay complex, looking north, *c.* 1905. The

former goods transit sheds are shown to the right. A tram passing over Monument Bridge in the distance completes the view.

A crowd of dockers gather to unload a cargo at the Riverside Quay to the south of Albert Dock, c. 1910. The photograph is by Marcus Barnard. Most of the predominantly wooden sheds were destroyed in the Second World War and were subsequently replaced by concrete structures in the late 1950s.

Another photograph by Parrish & Berry, this one titled 'Tide Time St Andrews Dock' and taken in late 1903. Locals gather around the entrance to St Andrew's Dock as a vessel manoeuvres through the lock gates with the swing bridge open in the background.

Thirteen
One for the Road

Most local historians have a fondness for one particular aspect of local history, and for many this is the study of local pubs, particularly those no longer with us. The author had amassed huge collections of images and ephemera relating to this topic, and has written extensively regarding the histories of those that interested him, including several books. The Dock Arms, formerely in Dock Office Row, was featured in a sketch made by the local artist F.S. Smith in around 1885, however, it seemed a photographic image of the building would never be found. The name of George Coverdale, who was in charge from about 1930, can be seen in this photograph, which also shows the former Queen's Dock whilst it was being filled-in. This would date the photograph to around 1933, although the pub had been in business since at least the 1780s. It was badly damaged during the blitz of 1941 and subsequently demolished.

Wincolmlee has had many pubs but only one of them had the misfortune to be located next door to a police station (see Chapter 10). The Sculcoates New Inn opened around 1830 and was located at Nos 59-60 Church Street (later re-numbered No. 269 Wincolmlee). The pub was situated near the junction with Swann Street and was one of many that were home to friendly society meetings, held in clubrooms on the premises.

The former Queens Hotel at No. 141 George Street re-opened in March 2002 as a nightclub called Pozition. Built as a private house in the late 1770s, when it was listed as No. 15 Charlotte Street, it was later the home and academy of the Revd J. Bird until around 1873. From around 1876 it became the Queen's Hotel, with its original entrance facing Charlotte Street Mews, as shown in this 1920s photograph.

The Darley Arms first opened around 1840; Robert Wharam, ale and porter dealer at the Darley Arms, No. 19 William Street on the corner of Great Thornton Street, was the first recorded licensee. The pub may have been named after the builder John Darley, as in this 1920s photograph Darley Place can be seen to the left of the pub. The pub now stands alone, drastically rebuilt, amongst more modern buildings of the 1950s and 1960s.

No. 6 Victoria Terrace Anlaby Road, originally a private house, had become the Argyle Hotel by 1858. The street opposite had been known as Asylum Lane after a lunatic asylum situated on its west side. The asylum closed around 1849 and the street was re-named Argyle Street in 1861 following complaints from residents. Argyle Street, therefore, may have been named after the pub. The Argyle closed in 1965.

The grand 1860s frontage of the Regent Hotel, latterly No. 31 Carr Lane, was built on the site of a much older inn known as the Unicorn. The Unicorn ceased to be listed in around 1860 and at that time Carr Lane was being redeveloped at this point. The Regent was first mentioned in a trade directory of 1867 when John Jackson, possibly the High Street wines and spirits merchant, was listed as the licensee.

Cotton Mill Street changed its name to Barmston Street in around 1863 after the nearby Barmston Drain. In 1872 William George Goring was licensee of the Barmston Hotel, No. 88 Barmston Street and in 1874 it was licensed as a six-day house. Situated at the corner of Lincoln Street and Barmston Street, the Hotel is shown here in the 1920s. The pub had been drastically re-fronted by the time of its closure in 1970.

The Pacific Hotel, situated at the corner of Fountain Road and Waterloo Street, was first licensed in 1873. Architecturally it was very similar to several other pubs in the area all of the same period, such as the East Central Hotel in Wincolmlee and the Crystal Hotel in Waterloo Street. It is seen here in a photograph of the 1950s. It closed in 1970 and was demolished soon after.

The present Ship Inn of 1931 replaced a much older inn, which had stood at the end of Ann Watson Street (formerly Hospital Lane) probably since the seventeenth century. The old inn was demolished and replaced by this French looking building with imitation half-timbering. The building is still in use and, along with its architecturally close relation the Endyke Hotel, is an excellent example of early 1930s pub architecture.

Although it was built only five years later than the Ship, the Anchor Hotel Southcoates Lane, of 1936, shows a complete change in architectural style. Its bold lines, still with a hint of Art Deco, are broken by its only decoration – castellated rainwater heads finished with embossed fleur-de-lis. The pub is still popular and relatively unchanged externally; known locally as Blue Heaven – one room was originally lit by blue lights.

This 1920s photograph shows the north side of Charlotte Street, and to the right, the entrance to Trippett Street. In the centre of the photograph is the Rowland Burden Inn, which had been a pub of some sort since at least 1791. The first known victualler was the fittingly named Robert Drinkall. All of the property in the photograph was demolished for the approach road to the new North Bridge of 1931.

The East Sculcoates Central Hotel is on the site of an earlier inn, the Sir John Falstaff, which was first recorded, in the eighteenth century. This early 1920s photograph shows the remodelled frontage of 1875, designed by architects Smith & Brodrick. 'Time' was last called in 1970 but the property survives, now vacant, at the corner of Green Lane and Wincolmlee.